Family Disciple Making

A Practical Guide to Raising Your Children as Disciples of Jesus

By James A. Lilly

world missions EVANGELISM

Copyright © 2020 by Jim Lilly

Family Disciple Making

A Practical Guide to Raising Your Children as Disciples of Jesus

by James A Lilly

ISBN: 9781703739220

Printed in the United States of America.

All rights reserved solely by the author. The author guarantees all contents are original and do not infringe upon the legal rights of any other person or work. The views expressed in this book are not necessarily those of the publisher. This work is made available under a Creative Commons Attribution-Share Alike 4.0 License (http://creativecommons.org/licenses/by-sa/4.0)

This work may be copied, translated, and modified, as long as all modifications and translations are made available to others under the same license. Copies of modifications and translations should be sent to jimlilly@yahoo.com.

Unless otherwise indicated, scripture quotations are taken from English Standard Version, © 2001 by Crossway

Endorsements

As I have traveled around the world and witnessed families among unreached people groups beginning to discover the Word of God for themselves, it struck me that there is a significant lack of family discipleship taking place in some of the most churched places on the planet. This book is invaluable in cultures where people have become reliant on pastors and priests to educate them one day of the week at best. Families walking together through Scripture and beginning to apply it to their lives would cause a revolution of peace and discipleship, and Jim provides wonderful insight in how to begin to do this in the pages of this book.
— **Pastor Josh Armstrong**, Vineyard Regional coordinator for Africa, Marysville, TN

After a lifetime of Christian ministry and disciple making, it is rare and delightful to have discovered this short book on family disciple making. *Family Disciple Making* captures the model of the New Testament where Jesus called others to "come alongside him" as he spoke, healed, confronted, and proclaimed the Kingdom of God. I would highly recommend this book to pastors, church leaders and especially Christian parents who have been directed by the Lord to raise their children in the truth of Jesus Christ. It is short, concise, to the point and overloaded with wisdom and practical skills to take anyone from being a novice to a fully mature disciple.
— **Rev. Tom V. Parrish**, www.toeternity.org Mendota Heights, MN

We now live in a society that makes keeping the family unit intact more difficult than any other time in history. Technology has created a vacuum that keeps the family apart, even as they share the same space within a home. Families can sit in the same room for hours and never communicate with each other as people are glued to computers, iPad, televisions, and smart phones. Statistics now show there is no difference with the divorce rate within the church and society as a whole. Jim Lilly does a masterful job of making this case within the first 2 chapters

In *"Family Disciple Making." h*e gives a simple step by step plan for families to come together as a family unit to discover God. Whether it be a traditional family unit, blended or single parent family, it allows the head of the family the opportunity to become the "Priest of their own household" rather than surrendering that responsibility to a youth Pastor or Sunday School teacher. The results will be the strengthening bond that will development between each family member, while becoming true disciples of Christ as God intended. If you have struggled with knowing how to bring your family together around God's Word, Jim has provided a road map on how to do it that is clear and straight forward. Any family that wants to take back their family from the high-tech world that has separated us should read this book.
— **Pastor Richard Williams**, President, Compassion for Life, Elkton, MD

Can family devotions be more than words going in one ear and out the other? Jim Lilly's *Family Disciple Making* gives parents tools to effect striking results:

Family Disciple Making

1. Bible reading becomes a group discussion, not a parental monologue.
2. Each adult and child designs a personal plan to obey the week's Scripture text in some practical way.
3. They each share the week's Bible story with someone outside the home, so that talking about God becomes a natural habit.
4. Each week the family finds a way to help a neighbor or friend in need.
5. When God answers their prayers for themselves and others, He proves He is not just a character in a book. He is real, and He is leading them into their destiny.
6. Parents, children, friends, and neighbors fall in love with Jesus and gladly become His disciples.

If you desire these results for your family, put into practice the principles of *Family Disciple Making*. Though the enemy will oppose every step forward, with perseverance "the God of peace will soon crush Satan under your feet" (Rom. 16:20).
— **Rev. Phil Bickel**, Author of *Disciple Maker: Fulfill Your Destiny in the Disciple-Making Movement Launched by Jesus Christ*, Minneapolis, MN

As I began my career as a pastor, I was responsible for a children's ministry of over 1,000 children from birth to 6th. grade. Later I directed an inner-city ministry to children who were at-risk in downtown Phoenix, AZ. We knew that the key to discipling children was the parents and that very little could be achieved during an hour on Sunday morning or during the week.

We realized that, when it came to the task of discipling their children, many parents did not know where to start. This book, *Family Disciple Making* addresses this problem and gives parents a practical way of doing it. It starts with having family Discovery Group Experiences. This naturally leads to an inmate relationship with Jesus and fruitfulness for His Kingdom. It both disciples the children and equips families to live as disciples of Jesus.
— **Pastor David Hinman**, DMM Specialist for Multiplying Vineyard Churches; Catalyst and Trainer with New Generations, Phoenix, AZ

Thank you so much for sharing this resource!
I have been praying for a couple of years to find a way to root my children in the Word of God. Every veteran mom has said they wished they had put Bible studies at the forefront of their homeschools. I just have not found the right way to do that. In my mind I thought I had not found the best "curriculum". Now I see that I just really did not know how to make disciples! This way of being in the scriptures is so authentic and approachable! I do not need another curriculum that tells my kids how to emulate a Bible character or teach them Latin and Greek. I just need to walk them through what it is like to read scripture and listen for God.
— **Mrs. Kate Milner** – Homeschooling mother of five boys from Blaine, MN, Just beginning family disciple-making

Contents

Contents

Acknowledgements iii

Introduction v

Chapter One - Raising Children in Today's World 1

Chapter Two - Raising Children from a Biblical Perspective 7

    Group Exercise 1: A Basic Evaluation 8

Chapter Three - Basics of the Discovery Process 11

    Written Discovery Studies 12

Chapter Four - Starting with Your Family 19

Chapter Five - Explanation of the Discovery Process 25

Chapter Six - Raising Children as Disciples of Jesus 35

    Group Exercise 2: Understanding the Disciple-Making Process 39

Chapter Seven - Applying Family Disciple Making to your Church 41

Appendices 42

    Discovering God Series 42

    Discovering Obedience Series 43

    Parables of Jesus Series 44

    Supplemental Reading: 45

Acknowledgements

This short book was birthed out of need and then discovering a wonderful resource.

Having raised five children, now watching my children raise their own, and seeing other parents attempt to raise their children, I am painfully aware of the challenges which parents face. I have seen the hard work of churches "educating children in the faith", yet also seen that all this work has rarely born the desired outcome – children who have a personal relationship with Jesus and carry that faith into their generation. These observations are shared by many parents and pastors. It was some of those who wrote the preceding recommendations, who actively encouraged me to complete and publish *Family Disciple Making*.

Additionally, I want to acknowledge my sister-in-law, Lonnie Ulmer who spent many hours proofreading and providing critical input for me to focus on the parents who will actually train their children. Roy Moran, founding pastor of Shoal Creek Church and author of *Spent Matches,* and *The Hybrid Church,* gave a further reorientation to the order and structure of the chapters. Phil Bickel, author of several books was the first to say, "you have to complete this and get it published soon." David Cross, pastor/missionary, provided an additional edit with suggested changes. Jim Yost, disciple-maker trainer and missionary church-planter in Indonesian, when he read a draft of the book wrote, "This is EXACTLY what we've begun doing here [in our church] with families! His experience with adapting it into the life of their church is reflected in the last chapter, "Applying Family Disciple Making to your Church". Then I want to thank the families with three to ten-years' experience using the Discovery Process with their families, who provided the practical advice that is given in Chapter Four. This book is an outgrowth of the experiences and input of many people.

Saving the best to last, I want to thank my wife Cindy who has supported me by relinquishing my time and attention, and then provided the final reading and editing.

Now, I want to thank you for investing your time and effort into Family Disciple Making. May it give you the joy of seeing your children grow as disciples of Jesus Christ with the ability and zeal to change their world by helping the kingdom of God come here to the earth.

Introduction

Parents have always faced a daunting task in preparing their children to function and thrive in a competitive world. For Christian parents this has become even more difficult. What were once called Christian countries and societies have become at first indifferent and now increasingly hostile to the basic truths of the Bible.

This book is intended to provide parents and churches with resources and tools to preserve faith, trust, and belief in God. Its larger purpose is to prepare parents and their children to transform their communities and eventually their countries. The Apostles of Jesus entered an extremely hostile world. Using what they had learned as disciples, they began slowly but surely to change their world. Within the geographic limits in which they operated; the apostles and the new disciples they made were successful.

Most of this book is designed to prepare you as parents, to be able to equip yourselves and your children with the same understanding and abilities as the families in the book of Acts. It will take some commitment, perseverance, and work, but you and your children will soon find yourselves living as effective disciples of Jesus.

How effective is this process? The parents of five sons who were among the first in the Midwest to start discovery studies with their children, wrote: "We see the discovery Bible study as the most powerful process we have ever encountered to help people gain the characteristics of disciples according the Word of God. This is the only thing we have ever done with our kids that they actually enjoy. And the fact that we all learn from God together is such a blessing. I love it when God uses my kids to teach me things I had not seen in the scriptures before.

Where to Start:
If you are ready to begin with your family, take a quick look at the Family Discovery Process on the next page and then go to Chapter Three where you will find an explanation of this process to use with your family. From there Chapters Four will give some practical advice on starting with your family. Chapter Five will give you a deeper understanding of the discovery process. Chapter Six will give you a foundation in what becoming a disciple meant to Jesus and how that applies to us today. Finally, Chapter Seven is written to church pastors and staff. It gives a brief verbal picture of integrating these families with the church structure.

If you are just looking and want to know why you should consider family disciple making, start with Chapter One. In it we will look briefly at what has happened to the United States, and how that has made the current model of church ineffective in its mission to the world. This has been most evident in its youth growing up and leaving the church. While the details of the story differ, a similar process with the same results has taken place in Canada and Europe.

Chapter Two will present a few of the Bible's instructions, admonitions, and warnings to parents. Group Exercise 1 of the chapter will give you as parents, an opportunity to evaluate what is currently happening with your children both at home and at church.

The Family Discovery Process

1) FAMILY UPDATES — Opening Questions:
- What are you thankful for this week?
- What challenges have you had this week?

2) SHARE EXPERIENCES — Review Questions:
- Retell the previous passage.
- To whom did you tell last week's passage? What happened?
- Did you do your "I will"? How did it go?
- How have you experienced God since the last time that we met?
- Report on the people you helped.

3) DISCOVERY — Bible Study: (Read, Reread, Retell, Details)

Each person in the family practices saying the passage in his or her own words. The **goal** is to learn together and be able to share this passage conversationally by memory, with someone outside the group.

Details: Discuss the passage:
- What happens in this scripture passage?
- What do we discover about God from it?
- What do we discover about people from it?

4) OBEDIENCE — "I Will" and "We Will" Statements

Identify what difference this passage makes in each of your lives.

I will change my daily life to reflect the reality that I have learned. (I will and the family will)

5) OUTREACH—Concluding Questions:
- What other questions do you have about this passage?
- With whom will you share this story, when, and how?
- Do you know anyone who needs help? What can our family do to help them?

Pray for the problems and needs of the family and for others you will share with and help.

Chapter One
Raising Children in Today's World

"Jesus loves me this I know for the Bible tells me so," is the first line of a Christian children's song that is familiar to most people raised in a Christian environment. For people born in the first half of the Twentieth Century, even those raised in non-Christian homes would likely be familiar with it. Today most children entering elementary school in this country are unfamiliar with these words. For them if they have heard of Jesus at all, his name is an expletive used in disgust or anger. The Bible is no more or perhaps less, familiar than the Quran.

The world has changed. From 1960 until 2010 American and Canadian societies moved from having a Christian orientation to a clear separation between popular society and Christianity. In the last quarter of the Twentieth Century the social norm was a professed neutrality toward Christianity. However, since 2010 the political and social environment has grown increasingly hostile toward Christian values and Christianity as a religion.

So how has this affected what the Church has been doing in teaching and training children? Based on the figures given by John Dickerson, in 2008 seventy percent of children raised in evangelical churches were not affiliated or attending church by age thirty.[1] If this continues, the future of the Church in America over the next generation is dark. In 2010, the weekly attendance of evangelical churches in America stood at less than nine percent of the American population.[2] Julia Quin reported that total church attendance of all denominations in 2008 was about eighteen percent on an average Sunday.[3] It doesn't take much imagination to see that the impact of failing to connect children both with God and the Church will lead to significant decrease in church

---

[1] John S. Dickerson, *The Great Evangelical Recession – 6 Factors that will Crash the American Church…and How to Prepare*, Baker Books, Grand Rapids, MI (2013), p. 103.

[2] Ibid i, p. 29

[3] Julia Duin – *Quitting Church – Why the Faithful are Fleeing and What to Do about it*, Baker Books, Grand Rapids, (2008), p. 44

membership. Looking at three generations, it can be projected that the Church will see more than an 80% reduction in membership in the next sixty years.[4]

---

[4] If each generation only retains 30% of its youth then 18% =11% = 3% = < 1%.

Breakdown between Society and the Church

How did all of this happen, and why has the Church not been able to reverse it? To understand this, we need to understand how Christianity became the official religion of Europe. The Church before A.D. 313 and after A.D. 380 was quite different in structure and operation. Before the Edict of Toleration by Emperor Galerius in A.D.311, the early Church in the Roman Empire operated as an oppressed religious system. Christians met in homes and secluded places. The Church still operated similarly to the book of Acts. Between the Edict of Milan in A.D. 313 and the Edict of Thessalonica in A.D. 380, the organization of the Church was integrated with the government of the State.

In this relationship, the Church provided moral direction to society and supported the State. The State for its part would put the Church's moral positions into law, and so supported the Church. Society applied both the moral teachings of the Church and the legal structure of the State. While this relationship existed, all was a harmonious whole. This amounted to a covenant between the Church, the State, and society. If the Church made proclamations about moral issues such as: fidelity in marriage, relationships between men and women and sex outside of marriage, the State would pass laws supporting these. Society, for its part, would put pressure on people to conform. Instruction came from the pulpit and application happened in everyday life. Together they functioned as something of a three-legged stool. This model proved to be very stable for more than 1500 years.

Civil and societal support of the Church broke down in Europe after the Second World War. In the United States it happened fifteen years later. The progression can be seen in a series of Supreme Court Decisions:

- Prayer – In 1962 the Supreme Court prohibited organized prayer as part of the school program. They drew upon a reconstruction of Thomas Jefferson's statement about the separation between Church and State. The First Amendment was originally intended to protect the Church from the State. Its new interpretation was that religion should be kept out of schools. This effectively meant that the Free Exercise Clause of the First Amendment to the Constitution of the United States, was to be interpreted to exclude religion from directly influencing the State.
- Abortion – The Roe vs. Wade decision in 1971 attacked the Church's commitment to treating "the least of these" as they would Jesus. The ruling violated much of the Church's understanding of the sanctity of life.
- Homosexual Marriage – No other decision so clearly broke the connection with Biblical values as the 2015 decision mandating that marriage include homosexuals. The basic concept of marriage as the union between a man and woman was overturned. This has led to a challenge

to the concept that God has authority to fix genders. It has also removed any legal basis for natural gender distinctions. This is illustrated by the transgender debates.

School policies and curriculum have been rewritten to implement these decisions and to indoctrinate our children. The moral teachings in the Bible are treated as bigotry and even the basic concepts of natural law are held in ridicule. The original covenant between Church and State was that the moral teaching of the Church would be supported. Now laws are made that are in direct opposition.

Popular media has impacted social culture and it too has also become largely hostile to Christianity. Moral values of sexuality and social responsibility have broken down.

The enabling and empowering agreement between Church, State, and society has been broken. The institutional structure that the Church has relied on has been largely rendered ineffective. When a moral position is given from the pulpit, it is no longer supported outside the walls of the church building.

How should the Church respond? There are three approaches that have been tried over the years. The first is to resist by every legal means possible. There are legal ministries that fight these changes in the courts. There are political ministries that are using political means to restore or at least resist these changes. Much of this effort relies on appeals to natural law. Until now, these have only been able to delay or partially divert the results of this fundamental shift.

A second approach was tried by the Church when Islam conquered and seized control of North Africa and the Middle East. The Church agreed not to resist or criticize the Muslim rulers or try to present the gospel. The rulers in turn agreed to allow the Church to exist, but each member would pay an annual tax for not being Muslim.

The Church turned inward seeking to strengthen its people in both traditions and the truths of the Bible. Using this approach, the Church survived in diminishing numbers for more than a thousand years.

Parts of the American Church are pursuing a similar approach by becoming inward focused and emphasizing Biblical fundamentals. While more and more people in the country are lost to Christ, many of these churches like the Church in the Middle East, in seeking to preserve their truths, have abandoned Jesus's mandate to make disciples of all peoples.

A third approach, which much of liberal Christianity is embracing, is to seek to promote the new morality. They seek to align themselves with the new "reality" of our society and government. In this way, perhaps they can maintain the supportive relationship with the State and society. Instead of steering the moral direction, they will fall in line with it.

Will any of these be successful? It is hard to see how they can be unless the connection between Church, State, and society can be reestablished. So, is there an alternative? When we look only at Europe and North America the outlook is discouraging. However, if we look to other parts of the world, is there something we can learn to do differently, something that is successful?

A Model that Works without Government Support

In the emerging Church of Africa and Asia, the gospel is spreading and the number of followers of Jesus is growing. As of 2010, the number of evangelical Christians was estimated at 180 million in Africa, 150 million in Asia, and 120 million in South America. North America was credited with 100 million and Europe with 6 million.[5] (This makes Europe the least evangelical continent on the earth.) The African and Asian churches, however, are growing faster than the population.

In 1949, Mao Zedong came to power in China. He expelled all the foreign missionaries. There was a great concern in the West that this marked the end of Christianity in China. God surprised everyone. Today, China has produced a Church that numbers between 60 and 100 million. Despite intense persecution this Chinese church is sending out missionaries to other lands. *(Please pray for the Church in China as the level of persecution has reached a new intensity.)*

India had been very resistant to the spread of the gospel, maintaining about two-percent Christian population from 1950 until 2005. Now, according to one mission group, the number of believers in Jesus has tripled and is about seven percent of the population. One 25-year-old movement in India headed by Victor Choudhrie baptized over one million new believers in 2012. Victor Johns heads another 30-year-old movement of more than 150,000 indigenous churches and according to a Hindu nationalist report, some twelve million believers in one of the most resistant areas in the country. Joy Punnoose heads a group of tens of thousands of new believers and church planters in another difficult area. There are many other church planting ministries and movements, as well.

Iran, a country hostile to Christians with no significant Church presence under the Shah, is now estimated to have about 3% of the citizens living as followers of Jesus.

In these places there is no support from the government and society. Both are frequently hostile. Is there anything we can learn from them? Where explosive growth is happening in the Church today, it is by the application of the Biblical principles that the early Church used. They have tapped into God's most important resources, the Bible and the Holy Spirit.

When Jesus appeared to the eleven disciples in Galilee after his resurrection, he first addressed the doubt that some had. Jesus affirmed that he had all authority in heaven and in earth. He instructed these disciples to make other disciples, baptizing and teaching them to obey all his commandments. Then Jesus made an important promise that in this effort of making disciples, he would be with them always, even to the end of the age (cf.

---

[5] James Forelines, Final Command Ministries, 2013 Mega Fest, Bo, Sierra Leone

Matthew 28:16-20). This is what characterizes these amazing movements in the rest of the world. Jesus is at work with ordinary people who obey his commands.

All these advances of the gospel have been met with opposition. Yet God continues to provide ways of advancing and extending the kingdom of heaven. It has come by looking at basic scriptural models. Models we can also use.

The Church in these countries has very little financial resources, but they know the most important things. They know the power of prayer. They know that God has given them the Bible and the Holy Spirit. And they know how to make disciples. In fervent prayer, they ask God how they should apply what he shows them in the scriptures. They look for opportunities to put what they learn into practice.

One of the most important elements in all these disciple making movements (DMMs) in Asia and Africa is that they are centered in the family. Large churches may grow up where persecution is low, but it is always the families who extend the kingdom of God. They pray for and reach other families with what they have discovered about God. It is this way that the good news of the kingdom and the hope that Jesus offers, is spread. The lives of these families change and that changes their relationships with the people around them. Many times, it is the attractiveness of these families, as well as the stories from the Bible they share, that produces a curiosity to learn what has happened to them. A family that is living as disciples of Jesus is equipped and able to show any new family how to discover Jesus in the Bible. It is a process of multiplication and replication.

The key to the restoration of America, Canada, and Europe is for families to live as disciples of Jesus. This means simply to obey his commands and share his Word with others. By training your children, you will be preparing your family to bring the good news of Jesus and his kingdom to your friends and neighbors. You will also be establishing each of your children in a faith and relationship with Jesus that will withstand all the pressures that society and government may place on them.

Chapter Two

Raising Children from a Biblical Perspective

How does God look at raising children? In Exodus 12, when God instructed Moses about the immediate things the Hebrew people needed to do to prepare to leave Egypt, he also gave instructions to teach the children in future generations. In Deuteronomy 6, God stresses that parents are responsible for the formation of their children. Here God instructs the parents to "inculcate or impress" (establish as a core understanding) the commandments of the Lord in their children. In Matthew 19, Jesus tells the disciples to "Let the children come to me, do not hinder them, for to such belongs the kingdom of heaven." These verses speak to both parents and community. Current statistics tell us that we must do a better job. The scriptures give guidance on how we can do this.

Proverbs 22:6

"Train up a child in the way he should go; even when he is old, he will not depart from it." This is a promise, but is it what the original language reads?

Dr. Douglas Stuart from Gordon Theological Seminary, as well as several Jewish Rabbis point out that in Hebrew, this verse is a warning not a promise. They translate it in similar ways, **"Allow an adolescent to grow up in his own way, when he is old, he will not depart from it."** The proverb is clear, unless you change the natural inclination of your teenager, as an adult he or she will not return to the ways of God.

As we mentioned earlier, seventy percent of children raised in evangelical homes are not walking with Jesus by the time they are thirty years old. These were children who regularly attended Bible-focused churches with their families.

Most parents expected the Church to lead their children to Jesus and establish them in a Christian life. In reflection, the Church usually taught children about God and Jesus and "*about* the way they should go." For most and maybe all of the thirty percent who were following the Lord as adults, somewhere they learned to walk *in* the ways of God.

It is most often at home that children learn to put into practice what God expects of them. There is quite a difference between being *taught about* and being *trained in* the ways of God. When we say "taught about" we mean the transfer of information. When we talk about being "trained in" we mean the ability to apply something effectively to a person's life with deep and practical understanding. They have had personal experience in what they were trained in, not just knowledge of a subject.

The challenge for as parents is, how can the children and adolescents in your home be established in the ways of God. How can they acquire the internal conviction and personal experience of the truth found in the Bible? How can they be fully equipped so that they continue to walk with God and even transform the society around them as they grow to adults?

The place to begin is to look at what you are doing now. What are you and your church doing to train your children in God's ways and where can you use some help?

Group Exercise 1: A Basic Evaluation

Whether you are a parent or a church staff member, take some time to think about and answer the following questions. If you are a parent, discuss this with your spouse. These questions are meant to help you evaluate and identify both weaknesses and strengths. As you discuss these questions together your understanding may change.

- What is "the way" that a child should go?

- Where can you find information and directions about this way?

- What is the difference between *training* a child *in* the way, and *teaching* a child *about* the way he should go?

Next take a few minutes to write down what your church does.

- What are some activities that your church does to <u>*teach* a child *about*</u> the way he should go?

10

Biblical Perspective

- What are some activities that your church does to *train* a child *in* the way he should go?

- What is the percentage of teaching verses training your children are receiving at church?

- What are some of the ways your church can do more to train your children "in" the way they should go?

Now look at your family.

- What are some activities that your family does to *teach* your children *about* the way they should go?

- What are some activities that your family does to *train* them *in* the way they should go?

- As with the church, what is the approximate percentage of teaching verses training?

- What are some of the ways you can do more to train your children *in* the way they should go?

- What percentage of your children's spiritual formation is happening at home verses at the church?

- How much of your children's spiritual formation should you delegate to the church and how much should you do?

- What limits you from doing a better job of training your children in the ways of God?

You may have questions about what to do, doubts about your ability, or do not know where to start. The remainder of the book will try to help you hear from God by giving clear perspective. Additionally, it will give you some tools that will enable you to train your children with ongoing evidence that they are experiencing God working in their lives.

In the next chapter you will be introduced to the Discovery Process. It will give you the basics of a family discipling process. As you follow this process with your family you will be increasingly immersed in the scriptures in a way that allows the Holy Spirit to teach you and your children in the way you and they, both should go. It will guide you into a much closer relationship with Jesus as his disciples.

The chapters that follow the introduction to the Discovery Process will explain it in greater detail giving you an understanding of what you will be trying to accomplish.

Chapter Three
Basics of the Discovery Process

Following is an outline for a complete oral family Discovery Study. Immediately following this is a description of a written study.

Each of these studies may be done at one time or done in parts as a daily devotion time of ten to twenty minutes. The normal pattern is to complete one scripture passage with a full study in a week.

Meet in a comfortable place where everyone can participate without distractions. The selected facilitator guides the meeting (See Chapter 5 for instruction for the facilitator). He or she should ask someone else in the family to record the challenges, discoveries, and application commitments. Everyone who is able should write down additional family discoveries about God and people.

1) FAMILY UPDATES — Opening Questions:
- What are you thankful for this week?
- What challenges have you had this week? *(Direct each person to look for an answer to their challenge in the passage to be studied. Record each person's challenge for review and prayer.)*

2) SHARE EXPERIENCES —Review Questions: *(Start these the second time you meet.)*
- Retell the previous passage. *(a goal is that each member of the family will have made each passage part of his or her life. Take an extra meeting if necessary, so that each person can tell the passage by memory and its lessons are implemented in the family.)*
- To whom did you tell last week's passage? What happened?
- Did you do your "I will"? How did it go?
- How have you experienced God since the last time that we met?
- Report on the people you helped.

3) DISCOVERY — Bible Study: (Read, Reread, Retell, Details)

Read the passage at least twice. The second time one person can reread it while the others just listen. Then take turns trying to retell the passage in each person's words. Make sure each person covers all the main points. *(Facilitator should ask questions that have the family repeat the dialogue of the passage as closely to the passage as possible.)* The **goal** is to learn together and be able to share this passage conversationally by memory, with someone outside the group.

Details: Discuss the passage: Participants are should confine their remarks to the passage being studied (no preaching or teaching or outside materials.) Challenge question: "Where does it say that in this passage?" (Children's questions in Chapter 5 on page 32 may be substituted for the following.)

- What happens in this scripture passage?
- What do we discover about God (or Jesus) from it?
- What do we discover about people from it?
- *(Facilitator may use additional key discovery and application questions to help family see important points.)*

4) OBEDIENCE — "I Will" and "We Will" Statements must be practical and able to be started in 24 to 48 hours. *(Record these for next meeting.)*

Now that the group members have discovered truths from God's Word, identify what difference this makes in each of your lives. The individual application "I will" statements, should be each person's response to what they discover personally and not directed by others. The group's "we will" statements should be by consensus of the entire group. Individual "I will" statements should happen weekly.

I will change my daily life to reflect the reality that I have learned. (I will)

- Based on what you have learned about God and people, how does it change what you should do?
- Did you find any answer to your challenging problem in the passage?
- **What will you change in your daily life?** *("I will...." - at least one thing weekly)*
- Is there anything we as a family should do? *(We will...." As things become apparent.)*

5) OUTREACH—Concluding Questions:

- What other questions do you have about this passage? *(Review the verses and clarify meaning).*
- With whom will you share this story, when, and how? *(Record these names for next meeting)*
- Do you know anyone who needs help? What can our family do to help them?

Pray for the problems and needs from the first section of the Discovery Process. Also pray for the people with whom you will share the passage and for those your family helps.

LAST QUESTION — Do we need to adjust when or how we do the next study?

Oral and Written Discovery Studies

Written Discovery Studies are wonderful for adults and older adolescents. For young children, discovery is about oral storytelling, drawing, skits, and songs, even building things with Legos and playdough. In short it is about engaging children's imaginations and play.

Oral discovery studies can be done while traveling in a car or hiking. They are much easier to fit into the nooks and crannies of the life of the most family of busy parents and children.

Even for families with older children, the actual family time of discovery is an oral process. Yet for those who are able to read and write and especially the person who will facilitate, preparing before the family time by doing a written study will give each person a longer period to think about the passage. Memorizing will usually go quicker, and more thoughtful discoveries can be shared.

For the facilitator, doing a written study can be a great help to determine the essential points that should come out during your family time. From these he or she can develop questions that will help the rest of the family learn important points. This can be as simple as having them look at key verses in the passage. Additionally, written studies can help facilitators plan how to help the family learn the dialogue of the passage. This may be to start saying a sentence or phrase and then have the other members complete it. The goal of dialogue questions is to prompt each person to anticipate the next words or thoughts.

If a child will facilitate the next study, it is helpful for a parent to help the child prepare a written study or coach him from his or her own study to think about the passage and develop questions to ask.

Some families may want to do the written studies together in a group. Generally, allow an extra half hour if you want to include it in your family time.

During the family time the notebooks with the written study, are used to record other discoveries about God and people, as well as challenges and things to pray about for other members of the family

Doing a Written Study

Transitioning children to writing is a process. It can begin with having the children write out one verse in a notebook and then draw a picture about the story. Do not let writing become a stumbling block to your family enjoying discovering the scriptures.

There are many ways to do a written Discovery Study. For people primarily interested in learning to tell a story, writing the story in your own words may be replaced by simply practicing saying the story. In this case you can copy the story from the Bible on the first of two facing pages and the write the lessons, application, sharing plan, and ideas for helping others on the facing page. Extra space on this page can be used for writing down discoveries, challenges, and "I will" and "we will" commitments you hear from others during the family discovery time.

Pick a style that is comfortable for you. Doing each step in the process is important, but how it looks and how each person writes it down is a matter of personal preference. For most people, the following process will produce the greatest long-term benefit.

Getting Started: For adults and older children, these written studies become a valuable resource to look back on later, so taking care to set up the pages will be helpful. Leave the first page as an index to record the passage reference and page number. This will help you find different studies. Then number every second page like the illustration of a Four Column Discovery Study.

If you fold the page lengthwise you can easily make two columns on each page as in the illustration, or four columns on the two facing pages

Written Study Format

Four-Column Discovery Study

First Sheet		Second Sheet	(Page #)
Copy Passage word for word as it is in the Bible	**Own Words** that I can share with others	**Lessons** Discoveries About God About Man	**Application** I will . . . We will. **Sharing Plan** Who will you tell? When? Where? How? **Helping Plan** Who needs help? What help is needed? What can be done?

A simple acronym: COLA, can be used to remember the essential components of a written discovery study. Copy, Own words, Lessons, and Application.

The First Column: Copy the Passage by Hand

In the first column, copy the passage by hand exactly as it is written in the Bible. This does a couple of things that helps you memorize. First, the process of writing something activates different parts of the brain. As you write, the passage is being fixed in the mind.

The second thing that happens by writing the passage word-for-word is that it forces you to look at each word individually. Words or phrases are noticed that were missed in the normal reading process. This can give deeper understanding of a passage.

The Second Column: Write (or say) the passage in your Own words

The next step is to write out the passage (or an outline) and / or practice saying it out loud, in your own words. Take some time to look at the sequence of the story. Is there action or movement? Identify all the characters in the passage and their relationship with each other. Consider what the motives of each person might have been. Can you retell it in your current context or in words that your children will be able to understand?

This will help fix the story in your mind and help you understand its meaning. In addition, the purpose is ultimately to be able to tell the story in your own words to someone else. For those who prefer to practice saying the passage out loud, writing this column can be skipped, but the goal of being able to tell the story remains the same.

Discovery and Application steps

The next two steps, the lesson/discovery step, and the application step, can be done in any order. Some may like to do the application step first.

The Third Column:

Lessons - The Discovery Step

The third step in the process is discovering what the Holy Spirit shows you in a passage. Write these down. You can note what you discover in each verse, or the things that impress you.

The family will add additional things when they meet, so leave room to record these. These discoveries will add to your own understanding. You will find that group learning is broader and deeper than that of any one person. Even the youngest member of the family will add insights and understanding.

There are three general questions to ask in this step.

1: "What is this passage about?"

When a passage includes a transitional word or phrase such as "therefore", "then". or "after this," it is helpful to read what happened before.

If you are struggling to understand a passage, be patient. When you meet as a family, another person may have an insight that will help clarify it. In the time between your written study and the family meeting the Holy Spirit will often give you understanding.

For parents of young children, as you are writing out the study, consider how you could encourage them to use their imagination in your family discovery time. Is there something they liked about the story? Is there something about the story or characters that they did not like? How can they find similarities in their own lives or in the lives of people they know? Could they act the story out or illustrated it?

2: "What have you discovered about God or Jesus or the Holy Spirit?"

For some passages, God's or Jesus's character, personality, purposes, expectations, commands, and promises are clearly revealed. For others, the answer may be more difficult to find. Do the best you can. Later when you meet with your family to search the passage, someone may look at it from a different perspective and be able to point out something that you had never seen.

If you are preparing to facilitate the time together, what are some questions that you can use to help the rest of the family look for the presence, character, or thoughts of

God or Jesus? Write them down to use during the family Discovery Study.

3: "What have you discovered about people?"

Sometimes, we learn something about human nature, pride, ignorance, how we relate to God, or each other. You may uncover sins to be avoided or examples to follow. The characters in a story often have attitudes and traits like us or people we know. All these discoveries will influence your understanding and your actions.

If you will be facilitating the family time, what did the characters of the story do? What might they have been thinking, or what caused them to do what they did? Develop some questions to ask that will have the family engage with the story.

For parents, can you help the children see similar character patterns, behaviors, or actions in other people or in their own lives?

The Fourth Column:

The Application — "I will . . ." step

The application step requires looking at the passage and deciding how you can apply what you have learned in your own life. Is there something you can change in your personal life, the way that you relate to God, or the way that you treat others? At first, it may be hard to come up with something that is practical and that you can report to your family the next week. It is a new way of thinking. The process becomes easier as you use it.

As you start, think of some ways that you can encourage you children to think about practical things they can do? Be careful you do not direct them into doing what you want them to do. Let each child take whatever steps he or she wants, to respond to what they have learned. Over a few weeks, God will lead them to work on even those things that you would like them to change. Often there are other things in their lives that need to change first. God sees deeper than we can.

Remember, we are trying to learn to be obedient, one step at a time. Look at the way God deals with us. If he were to bring everything before you and say, "Change!" you would be overwhelmed, and the task would be impossible. God has placed all of us in families to learn how the natural training process works. Every Olympic athlete started life as a baby. As he began to crawl and then walk, he received encouragement from his parents and siblings. Years of support from his family and coaches resulted in winning an Olympic medal.

This is what obedience-based Disciple-Making is all about.

Obedience-based Disciple-Making is all about a decision to change a direction or part of your life. You begin with a small *measurable* step. These steady changes fulfill what Jesus meant when he said, "Repent (*change the way you think and act*) for the Kingdom of heaven is at hand" (Mark 1:15). Being a disciple of Jesus is a life of regular Spirit-directed obedient change, resulting in a deepening love for Jesus (John 15:10).

Take a few minutes to write out an "I will" statement. Then ask yourself, "In a week, can I clearly report whether I did it or not?"

During the first few meetings with your family, evaluate how practical each of the "I will" statements is. Encourage each other with practical suggestions. Younger children may need more time and coaching to learn how to do this.

Sharing the passage:
This is also the column to identify a person with whom you could share the passage. Ideally this would be an individual who would be interested in the story. If no one comes to mind, then choose someone you expect to see in the next few days. (Again, younger children may need some help with this.) Write down where and when you expect the meeting to take place. How would you start the conversation and transition to telling the story? Next, what follow-up questions could you ask? Finally, ask God to direct you. Even if events do not go as you planned, the fact that you have a plan will improve how you share and increase the chances that you will be successful.

Who can you help?
Ultimately this is a family decision, but by considering this question before you meet, you will have some time to gather information about the need and possible ways of helping.

Does everyone have to do a written study?
The oral family discovery study is the core of the Discovery Process. While doing a written study is desirable and improves the quality of the sharing, it is not possible for younger children. People in your family who do not read well can be expected to do everything orally. Whether you write it or just listen to it, learning the passage by memory is essential.

In Summary
There are six steps in this written Bible study process:

1. **C**opy the passage as it is written in the Bible, including verse numbers.

2. Write the passage in your **O**wn words.

3. Write the **L**essons you discover about the passage, about God, and about man.

4. Write how you **A**pply what you learn by writing one or two "I will" statements.

5. Write out your plan to share the passage with someone.

6. Write a suggestion of who your family can help.

Chapter Four

Starting with Your Family

Each family will be different. You may have young children, older children, or a spread of ages. You may be homeschooling, sending your children to a Christian school, or public school. Your children may be excited to start this, they may be hesitant, or they may be defiant. Your children may identify strongly as Christians, they may not think much about it, or they may be rejecting your faith. You may be a multi-generational Christian family, an intact father-mother couple, a blended family, or a single parent. You may be part of a supportive church or support group, a church without close fellowship, or even with no church home. How you start and implement the Discovery Process will need to be adjusted for your unique situation. Here are some ideas to help you get started.

Before you start with your entire family, do at least two and preferably four Discovery Studies with another adult. It takes about four or five times of doing complete studies to become comfortable with the process. Start by reviewing and discussing this manual with each other. In particular, read through the Discovery Process Questions at the beginning of Chapter Three. Next, on the internet, watch the two videos at the following URLs (active as of 2020):

Dave Hunt — Group Process (4 min.):
https://www.youtube.com/watch?v=dHggzCWYL-Q or www.bit.ly/DHGroupProcess

Dave Hunt — Bible Study Process (5 min.):
https://www.youtube.com/watch?v=azJq4McK7uc or www.bit.ly/DHBible

In a notebook write out the first discovery study and then go through the first practice Discovery Study with a partner. If you have questions, review this manual and the videos. Once you are comfortable with the Discovery Process, you are ready to introduce it to the rest of your family.

You know your children best, so develop a plan to introduce the Discovery Process to them. It is important to remember that each child will have a different response based on his or her unique personality.

You can be flexible on how much time you spend together and how many verses you work on each time you meet. Look for times you already get together. Meals, bedtimes, or family devotions are easily added to or rearranged. Regardless of how you divide the studies, attempt to complete one discovery study in one or two weeks. There is a balance. It is important to keep momentum in your studies. It is also important to thoroughly understand what you are studying.

The "I will" and telling someone else parts will be uncomfortable at first. But with experience, the results become the most important and enjoyable parts of the studies. As you begin, do not be discouraged. You will see that after four or five times the whole process will become familiar. With your children, talk about ways to complete both the, "I will," and how to share the passage portions of the process. Be understanding if family members do not complete their "I will" commitment or fail to share the passage every week, but make sure that they try each time. As you start, lead by example.

After the third or fourth study, if your children are older, discuss with them what you could do to make the studies go better. For younger children, look for things that are hard for them. Try changing those parts. Then asking, "Do you like this better?"

In a Discovery Study, Jesus by means of the Bible and the Holy Spirit, is the teacher. You and your children are all learning from him.

Except for leaving out parts, you can change the order of anything. Remember that when you sit down to do a Discovery Study, Jesus by means of the Bible, and the Holy Spirit, is the teacher and you the parents and your children, are all learning together. You are all to be supportive as one brother or sister to another. Together, you can make these Discovery Studies work best for your family, even as schedules change.

Your First Discovery Studies:

You can do Discovery Studies on any scriptures. If your church is doing a sermon or teaching series, you can do Discovery Studies on the passages that will be used the next week. The following four passages will help your family understand the reasons for the Discovery Process.

Passages for understanding the process.

Matthew 23:8-11 – Jesus is the teacher and we are all brothers

John 14:15-21 – If you love Jesus you will obey him, and the Father will send the Spirit.

John 14:22-26 – Jesus and the Father will make their home and the Holy Spirit will teach.

Deuteronomy 6:4-9 – The Shemah, Love God, teach your children and speak of him.

Once your family has completed these first four passages, the next two discovery series, "Discovering God" and "Discovering Obedience", which are in the appendices will both lay a firm foundation in understanding Jesus and his mission and prepare your family to share with others who may not have any knowledge of the God of the Bible. With young children the "Parables of Jesus" are a good place to begin. They are fun to act out and easier to memorize.

There are additional discovery series in *Great Commission Disciple Making* which is described in the Supplemental Reading section found on the last two pages of this book

Practical Family Focus:

In the simplest, there is a hierarchy of four things that each and all children need to know[6]:
1. They are safe
2. They are loved
3. They are unique and respected
4. They are responsible

This is true in any culture at any time. A family engaged in discipling their children will establish all four of these.

- As each member shares the difficulties in his or her life and the family address them, it establishes a **safe** and secure environment.
- Praying for and helping each person in the family builds a sense of care and **love**.
- Listening with **respect** as each person shares what they learn from a passage builds appreciation for his or her **uniqueness**.
- Finally, the expectation that each person will take some action based on what has been studied and to share with others, coupled with accountability, builds **responsibility**.

In the midst of day-to-day life, it is common for parents to fail to see the God-size responsibility and opportunity with which we have been entrusted. To give a perspective to this responsibility, Jesus enumerated three commands. He said living a life pleasing to God flows from the first two: "Love the Lord your God with all your heart, soul, might, and mind"; and "Love your neighbor as yourself".

The last one, "Make disciples of all the nations" usually called the "Great Commission", is directly connected to loving your neighbor. It is key to seeing God's kingdom come to the earth. This final command is also the doorway of opportunity for your children's future. It is the culmination of Jesus' work on the earth with his disciples.

Loving and obeying Jesus is the essence of being his disciples.

The application of what we learn to our own lives and sharing the stories with others, gives each member of the family opportunities to see God at work and experience his love.

> "Whoever has my commandments and keeps them, he it is who loves me. And he who loves me will be loved by my Father, and I will love him and manifest myself to him."
> John 14:21

Individually sharing what you learn and as a family, helping others, are practical ways of loving your neighbor as yourself. When anyone in your family helps another person start the discovery process with their family, your family is participating in the Great Commission.

Family disciple making will be new to you. Fortunately, there are families that have gone ahead. On the following pages is some of their advice.

---
[6] Randy Torpen, Common Ground Consultants

Advice for families just starting from those who have gone before:

Josh and Amanda Armstrong, Marysville, Tennessee (Two children, ages 7 and 10; Three years of Family Discovery Studies):

Josh
- Teaching the kids how to ask the questions themselves, and how to organically facilitate the conversations has been good.
- Also, getting the kids to see our neighbors as God sees them, and how to identify persons of peace has been especially interesting.

Amanda
- "It has been wonderful to brainstorm with our children to find fun and unique ways to engage with the other families around us. What we are learning as we discover the Word of God together as a family becomes alive when we begin to have spiritual conversations with people in our neighborhood and schools."

Mike and Sarah Neterer and their children, Minneapolis, Minnesota (Three son ages 12 to 19, Eight years of Family Discovery Studies) :

Sarah:

- It is important to give the children ownership and allow and encourage them to take turns leading when they are able and want to.
- Set a time and duration for the family discoveries studies. Stick to it unless the children want to go longer. Keep your word.
- Flexibility and opportunistic: Do it while driving, on vacation, when out on the lake, do at dinner time. Take advantage when the children's friends are over.

Children input:

- When Caden had a college friend over for dinner, the friend said, "that is the best Bible study I have ever been part of. It is the first time that someone was not talking 'at' me."
- When asked what they like best, they said, "it includes everybody in the group, and it gives freedom to explore and discover".
- They also said, "stick to the script as written, the questions are good, but going off on a tangent is not always bad." (Sarah added, "We need to let the Holy Spirit lead when he decides to.")
- They added, "it good to have us children lead it, but it is good to have an adult facilitate it sometimes."

Mike:

- The trick is obedience. Checking to see that they are following through on their commitments is a place I fail. There was one time recently when one of the sons was convicted about what the family studied and came to me to repent.
- After eight years of it we are still seeing the fruit. We are sticking with it.

Starting with Your Family

David Cross, :Burlington, Wisconsin (Five children, ages 13 to 19; Ten years of Family Discovery Studies)

- Include the whole family, but do not expect younger ones to sit through the whole thing. We approached this in a flexible way and asked each of the kids the questions, but if they stepped away to play with toys (under five years old), we were fine with it. We found that they naturally gravitated back to the table to join us as the meetings went on.
- One way to engage kids five years old and older is to assign one of them the role of facilitate the study. They ask the questions. Each one of our kids loved asking the questions. Also, they could help keep the group on subject by asking clarifying questions such as "Where do you see that in the text?"
- Choosing a Bible translation for the youngest person should be a least-common-denominator. For example, the NLT may be the best translation for younger folks. The CEV is specifically written for readers of English as a second language.
- In the process of retelling the story, we often acted out the story as a family. That kept all ages involved.
- Even though we went through one lesson each day, we only asked the obedience questions on Sundays. That way, we would have time to do the thing the Lord was telling us and to tell the people the Lord brought to mind.
- The Discovery Study questions can be used for any devotional study which is important for kids to recognize. The point of asking these questions is that we are not simply to absorb information. Rather, when they read a teen devotional, for example, they are interacting with the Word of God and they should be thinking, "What is God telling me to do about this? Who needs to hear this?"
- For kids younger than five, we would often take out some of their toys to have them act out the story with their own toys.
- Kids can also draw the story as it is being read. This will help those children who cannot read to identify the important parts and interact with the text.
- Often, we had to encourage the kids to think of *different* people to tell each week. Their inclination was just to tell their closest friends.
- By the time the kids were 9-10 years old, we began to ask the kids whether the people they told about the story might like to do a Discovery Studies themselves. Rather than incorporate their friends into our study, they started new Discovery Studies with their friends. Soon, their friends' parents and grandparents were asking questions about the Discovery Studies and got involved as well.
- When children come up with life questions, rather than just answering the questions for them (even from the Bible), we would open the Bible with them to the passage we would have otherwise explained. We would do a quick Discovery Study with them asking the same questions. Incidentally, this is the same way I would mentor leaders in the 55 churches we saw in our Iranian movement.

Kurt and Carrie Olson, Almond, Wisconsin (Five sons, ages 19 to 28, Eight years of Family Discovery Studies):

Kurt

- While doing the discovery study treat children as your equals - Holy Spirit will speak through them. What they hear is as valid as what you hear. You will learn from what children share as much as they will learn from you.
- You walk a tightrope between encouraging and requiring obedience. Remember children are usually not volunteers when you first start. The process and their involvement in it are dynamic and changing.
- Let children facilitate when they are able and want to. Give them some control in the family studies.
- Celebrate when God demonstrates himself in, to, and through the children. Do not lose the opportunity to acknowledge their experience with God. I regret that I did not do more of this.
- Look at the interest level of children. Ask involvement and permission when making changes. Let them have a say.
- Seasons of life - be willing to retool as things change. Watch what is going on with each of them. Ask questions and talk about how the studies are going.
- We did the written study around the dining room table. We only asked the opening questions once or twice a week. There were lots of oral only studies.
- How many verses per study? Usually do no more than ten verses. However, when doing stories, the passages can be longer, as many as 15-20 verses.

Carrie

- Keep it simple. It is about each child experiencing God, not teaching the children.
- You are not the teacher. Let them see that they can do it too.
- Best discussion happens when children lead.
- Let the children get into the Word.
- There is a big difference between teaching and training. We train by having everyone put what they learn into practice.
- Strong willed children need a challenge. It can be a challenge to lead the family studies or it can be to share with another person or start a study with someone else.
- Transition into adolescence - always couple independence with responsibility - Don't tell them you are doing this but have this focus.
- Keep it enjoyable: morning coffee, snacks, special treat for Discovery Study times. Set the right environment. This changes with the children's age.
- Small children are concrete learners not analytical.
- The sooner they can experience God the better.

Chapter Five

The Purposes of the Steps of the Discovery Process

Defining Biblical Terms

Before explaining the purposes of each of the steps of the Discovery Process, it will be helpful to have a working understanding of some common Biblical terms and phrases.

Repentance is the translation of the Greek word Μετανοια (Metanoia). It means a change of mind that results in a change of action in and direction of, a person's life. In practice, it means obeying from the heart, everything that God tells us. Just as Jesus tells us in John 14:15, "If you love me you will keep [obey] my commandments," and Matthew 28:19 "teaching them to observe [obey]all that I have commanded you." Repentance is the prerequisite to enter the kingdom of God. For our use, it is understood as an ongoing process of conforming our lives to the words of the scripture as revealed and directed by the Holy Spirit (Romans 12:1 and 2; John 14:26).

Grace: is not explicitly defined in the Bible, but a working definition can be constructed from the verses in John 14:15-26. The definition that is understood in the Discovery Process is that it is *the presence and power of God working in us and through us to accomplish his purposes for his glory.*

Jesus is Lord: Romans 10:9 says that, "If you confess with your mouth that Jesus is Lord and believe in your heart that God raised him from the dead, you will be saved." Confessing Jesus is "Lord" refers to an ongoing activity. It means we have lived for some time obeying him.

The Good News: Jesus presents the good news as "the kingdom of God is at hand" and Acts adds that it is realized in Jesus. (Matthew 4:17,23; Acts 5:42).

Bringing the kingdom to earth is the central task that Jesus gave his disciples. We affirm this with our lips every time we pray the Lord's prayer.

> "'…Our Father in heaven,
> hallowed be your name, your
> kingdom come, your will be done,
> on earth as it is in heaven.'

— Matthew 6:9-10

In this prayer Jesus left us with a vision for the world; a purpose for living; and a mission to accomplish God's objective for the world.

- **Vision:** "*Our Father in heaven*"; that every man, woman, and child would have an intimate relationship with God as their father. This is a unique relationship with God that no other people share, other than those who call upon Jesus and obey Him as their Lord.
- **Purpose:** "*Hallowed be your name*"; that God would be honored. Any person can honor God with their words, but a child whether he is small or grown, honors his or her father by all he does as well as by what he or she says. There is a special intimacy of a child and father and father with child. God is most fully honored by those who call him Father.
- **Mission:** "*Your kingdom come*"; bringing God's kingdom to earth. This is the uncompleted work of Jesus. He left this mission first to the twelve disciples. Then through them and the records they left, he left it to those of us who follow. He promised to all his disciples who set themselves to make disciples, that he would be with them to the end of the age (Matthew 28:20).

  The good news of Jesus is not just that we will get to go to heaven, but that we get to participate in bringing the kingdom of heaven to earth.
- **Objective:** "*Your will be done on earth as it is in heaven*"; When God's kingdom comes his will is done on earth. History has given us examples of the Kingdom of God being manifested on earth. Wales in the early 1900s, towns in Guatemala in the 1980s, and towns in Cuba the last few years. Jails are empty, families are healthy, people are prosperous. All of this is the result of lives being changed and God's will being done on earth.

The Discovery Process

For smaller children or others in the family who have difficulty reading and writing, others can help them learn the passages. For small children, the passages selected may need to be adjusted and the questions that are asked, tailored to meet the child's abilities.

The Discovery Process is made up of five sections each with a set of questions. They can be grouped into three parts: Look back at what has happened; look upward to what God wants to show you; and look forward to what God wants you to do.

- Building Family – Opening Questions – Look back at what each person has experienced.
- Share Experiences – Review Questions – Looking back at what each person has done and how God has responded.
- Discovery – Bible Study (Read, reread, retell, details) – Looking to

what God will show each family member as you study his word.
- Obedience – "I will" and "We Will" Statements – Looking forward to what each member of the family is going to do with what they have learned.
- Outreach – Concluding Questions – Looking outward to reaching others.

The entire process can be completed in a single sitting on a weekly basis or spread throughout the week as a daily devotional. As the family grows and demands change, the process can be adapted. But it is important that each step be completed. In general, try to complete one scripture passage a week.

However, the goal is to make each passage part of the lives of each family member. In some cases, you may want to extend the time you spend learning and implementing the lessons of a passage.

Each step is important in the disciple-making process. But the **key parts** of the disciple-making and Great-Commission aspects of the process are **obedience** and **"telling-others"** parts.

Role of the Facilitator:
The discovery process relies on the scriptures and the Holy Spirit to do the teaching (John 14:26). There is no leader in the traditional sense, who teaches and directs. Rather each week the family should select a person to facilitate the next study. Normally one of the parents assumes this role until everyone in the family is familiar with the process. Then families are encouraged to rotate the duties of being the facilitator among all the family members who are able. This may involve parents and older siblings coaching younger children *(about eight years old is generally the age when children can begin to facilitate.)*

The facilitator is one of, and equal to the others in the study. The facilitator, however, has certain responsibilities. He or she:

- Prepares before the family Bible study. This includes being able to ask questions to guide the rest of the family to discover the most important part of the passage.
- Maintains order. Makes sure that each person contributes to the discoveries and that no one dominates the discussion.
- Makes sure that each person can tell the story to another person. *(Having people practice in pairs and role-playing can assist this.)*
- Makes sure that all comments relate to the passage during the discovery step, and that there is no teaching or preaching. This applies to the facilitator as well. The other members of the family should hold each other accountable to this.

  (Anyone can ask, "Where does it say that in this passage?")

- If there are small mistakes in answering the questions about the passage, the facilitator should not make them an issue. But if there are statements that do not seem to be related to the passage, the facilitator should ask the person to explain where or how they see that in the passage. This both helps keep the study on course, but can lead to deeper discovery and understanding.

- Selects a person to record a list of each person's challenge and "*I will*" and any of the group's *"we will"* statements. This list should be used during the next meeting.
- Is an active participant in all the parts of the process as an equal.
- *When a child leads: depending on the child's abilities, a parent should coach him or her both during preparation and as he or she leads the meeting.*

Guidelines for a Discovery Study: The Bible and the Holy Spirit are the teachers. This means all comments must come from the passage being studied and each person should respond to what he or she has learned, to determine what he should put into practice in his or her life.

Only discovery; no teaching or preaching during a Discovery Study

During each study, the focus is entirely on discovering directly from the passage. There is no teaching, preaching, or bringing in outside materials. Each person should share only what he or she discovers in this passage. There are several reasons for this:

- First, it allows the family to complete the process in a reasonable amount of time.
- Second, it keeps everyone equal. If anyone brings in outside material, it may intimidate some of the others and they will not share freely.
- Third, it helps the entire family learn together. The younger children will discover simpler and age appropriate ideas from the passage. Older members of the family will contribute more complex thoughts. Each person will have a unique perspective on the passage. In this way the family will learn together. It allows the family to get the most out of the passage.
- Fourth, it prevents going off on tangents or confusing the study with non-Biblical ideas.

There is a challenge question that any member of the family can ask if they do not see a connection between what one person said and the passage they are studying. Anyone can ask, *"where does it say that in this passage?"* This both keeps each family member focused on the passage and it also assures that each person understands the reasoning of the other person's comments. This is another way that the entire family learns together.

One mother described her experience with the Discovery Studies, "The hardest thing for me at first, was not saying anything when my sons didn't see what I thought was obvious. I wanted to teach them what was there. It was especially difficult as I listened to my youngest son, who would only pick out the most obvious things. Then I realized that he was learning what his young mind could handle. As each older son shared, the level of discovery went deeper and deeper, until when my turn came I had very little to add."

Reflecting on previous passage studies is encouraged, but do not refer to passages which are not familiar to everyone in the group.

The **OPENING QUESTIONS** are designed to deepen communications between family members.

- What are you thankful for this week?

This question takes everyone's minds off problems and other activities. It encourages everyone to listen to each other and recall the good things that have happened recently.

- What challenges have you had this week?

When sharing challenges, the natural tendency is for others to offer advice. This will lead the family off the study and use up the time. It is better to write down what people identify and have them look for an answer in the passage. This will allow the Holy Spirit and the scripture passage to provide direction. Finding answers this way will allow your family to experience the Holy Spirit working. These challenges are also things the family should pray for or plan to help with, at the end of the meeting.

SHARE EXPERIENCES – The Review Questions: These are started during the second meeting. Giving an account of what each person does provides an incentive to fulfill what each person has committed to do. Accountability is an essential part of the discipling process.

- Retell the previous passage.

A goal is that each member of the family will have made each passage part of their life. Do not feel bound by a schedule. It is not as important to complete a list of passages as it is that each person knows each story well and its lessons are applied to your family.

- To whom did you tell last week's passage?

Sharing experiences and asking for and giving suggestions to one another on how to improve, is important as you begin doing this. Telling others will be a new skill for most of you. It gets easier and can help form new or deeper relationships with the people you meet and interact with. Most importantly, it gives the Holy Spirit an opportunity to use you to work in another person's life.

These sharings can also be very encouraging, when things happen that show that God is actively involved with your family members. For example:

The mother I mentioned earlier told me of one son who shared a passage with a friend at school. As the two discussed the passage the friend told her son that he was thinking about suicide. The son was able to get him to a counselor. In a few weeks, the friend and his family began attending church.

In one training session, a woman told us that her "I will" statement was that she would visit a neighbor. The two had been close friends, but they had a serious argument and had not spoken for two years. The woman made a special dish for her neighbor and brought it over. She knocked on the door. She said she wondered if her neighbor would even answer the door. The neighbor did come. As they talked, the woman asked her neighbor's forgiveness for the hurt she had caused. The neighbor broke out in tears and poured out her heart, telling her how much she had missed their friendship. When the neighbor asked the woman about her life. She told her neighbor about what Jesus was doing in her life, and why she had come. The neighbor asked the woman to pray with her to receive Jesus. The story really encouraged us all.

- Did you do your "I will"? How did it go?

You will need to encourage each other as you begin. Was the "I will" commitment too ambitious? Was it too vague?

- How have you experienced God since the last time that we met?

God is at work all around us and often in us. Learning to recognize God's presence and influence leads to a greater "awareness of God."

- Report on the people you helped.

This is a time to identify additional needs of the people you help. Helping others is also a time of discovery, of learning more about others and of building relationships.

THE DISCOVERY STUDY is the heart of the Discovery Process. It requires each person to draw conclusions based only on the information found in a specific passage.

The Discovery Study is designed to guide individuals in small groups to discover the basic truths about God, his kingdom, and man's relationship to both. It uses just one source, the Bible, without any distraction from outside sources.

Basic Discovery Questions:
- The first question in the study is, "What is this passage about?"
- The last two questions are:
  - "What do we discover about God?" and "
  - What do we discover about man?".

These simple questions are designed to lead us to change our thinking and understanding according to what the Holy Spirit shows us in the Bible.

The first few times answering these questions about God and man may be difficult, especially for younger children. The set of Alternate Questions for children on page 30 may be an easier way to start.

The Discovery Process

Learning Passage by Memory

STEP ONE: The Discovery Study starts by each person becoming able to tell the passage in their own words from memory. One person tells or reads the passage outloud two times. The first time everyone who can read, follows along in their own Bible. The second time, the others close their Bibles and simply listen to understand it in their minds.

STEP TWO: The next step is for the facilitator to go through the entire passage a third time using dialogue questions. These questions ask the group to recall what happens in the story, not what they learn. They focus on identifying characters and completing sentences and thoughts. These can be tailored and are especially useful when your children are young.

Further discovery questions can ask the family to discuss what they think motivated the characters of the story or what they were thinking. These questions are meant to help each person both learn and understand the passage.

STEP THREE: After this, each person, in turn, should try to say the passage by memory. *(in larger families, you can break into smaller groups of two to four to practice.)* Use words and expressions to retell the story that others will understand when you share it. *(With young children, the retelling can be very simple.)* As one person says the story, the rest of the family listens. As they listen, parts they missed or have forgotten will be recalled and reinforced. This is a key part to the rapid memorization possible in group learning.

As a rule, after people have heard the passage spoken by memory five or six times, the entire family will have the passage committed to memory.

After each person retells the story, the facilitator can ask the family to identify parts forgotten. It is helpful for the facilitator to tell the story correctly after each one or two attempts to retell the story. People will repeat what they have most recently heard, so giving them an accurate version will be helpful.

Emphasizing parts of the passages with gestures or actions, putting the story to song, acting out the story, or drawing pictures to illustrate it, are all effective ways to help commit the passage to memory. *(With smaller children, simplifying the language of the passage as you retell it can be helpful.)*

Word-by-word memorization of a passage can be intimidating. Recall that in the three synoptic gospels: Matthew, Mark, and Luke, many of the same stories appear, but rarely are they identical. Each disciple learned and deeply understood these stories. They accurately retold them in the appropriate context. As you think about telling the passage to someone else, consider using words and terms easily understood.

Why be able to tell the passage by memory?

- First, there is a scriptural promise, "So faith comes from hearing, and hearing through the word of Christ" (Romans 10:17). This works both as we ourselves hear a passage and for others as they hear us tell it.

- Second, it is our goal to have each person make the passage part of their mind and life so that the Holy Spirit can both teach us and to call it to remembrance as needed in our lives (John 14:26).
- The third reason is that each person is expected to pass it along to at least one other person each week. *(Family members will need coaching depending on their abilities.)*
- Finally, retelling each passage or story prepares the family to discuss it.

Memorizing becomes easier with practice. There are many people who are certain that memorizing is impossible for them. They all find that it <u>is</u> possible and that it gets easier the more they do it. Do not let fear hinder you. As a family you are doing this together.

This process of learning to tell the passage by memory can become a time of family creativity. Especially with younger children, acting the passage out, having family members take roles and say lines can be fun. Other ideas with children include having family members do a puppet show or choosing two teams and having competition between them. Drawing pictures, even if they are stick figures to illustrate the story and then using them to retell the story can be helpful. Remember the goal is to be able to tell others as well as learn it yourselves.

Once each person in the family can tell the story in his own words, you are ready to discuss the story answering three basic questions:

- What is the story about?

This includes a literal understanding of the story and applying it to our lives or the lives of those who heard it directly from Jesus. What does the story illustrate?

- What do you learn about God?

This would include what we learn about Jesus or how this passage points to Jesus. Often as you answer the question about people, it will cast some insight into the nature of God.

- What do you learn about people?

What is the passage telling us about the people of the time and people today? What behavior is the passage pointing to? What does the passage tell us about how we should relate to God and other people?

The following list of questions for children are examples of different discovery questions that can be used.

Alternative Sets of Questions:

<u>Children (and Oral Learners)</u>: For studies with younger children, discovery questions like the following ones can be used in place of the basic three:

- What do you like about the story?
- What individuals or groups are in the story?
- What did you learn about each of them?
- What do you think they were thinking about? Why did they do what they did?
- How did you see God or Jesus in the story?
- What applies to your own life from the story?

THE OBEDIENCE – "I will" and "we will" section is the application part of the process.

- Based on what you have learned about God and people, how does it change what we should do?

This is a time for each person to respond to what the Holy Spirit has shown them in the passage.

- Did you find any answer to your problem in the passage?

Often the Holy Spirit will reveal a new way of approaching a person's challenge even when the passage has nothing directly to do with it.

- **What will you change in your daily life?** *("I will...." - at least one thing weekly)*

The purpose of this section is for each family member to respond to what they have learned by making a small practical and measurable change in his or her life that can be accomplished in a week.

- Is there anything we as a family should do? *(We will...." As an opportunity arises.)*

This may include how you relate with one another or as a family, treat others, or live out your life as a family.

Remember: it is the Holy Spirit who must prompt the response in each family member. Each one is to make an "I will" statement for each passage studied. Parents may want their children to make certain changes in their lives and children may want their parents or siblings to make changes, but it is the Holy Spirit who is in charge. This means that each person should develop their own "I will" statement without prompting of anyone else. These "I will" statements must be specific, and each person should be doing them by the time your family starts a new study. *(The family will need to coach one another as you begin, especially with younger children.)*

THE OUTREACH – Concluding Questions will bring your family discovery time to a close.

- Is there still something you do not understand about the passage?

First, we want to be sure that each person understands the passage. It is not unusual after the discussion, for people to have thought of some new questions or not understand something. Since in this section, each person should decide to whom they will tell the passage, everyone should be comfortable with the passage.

Look at verses that are not clear. Children particularly may need something to be restated in terms they can understand.

- With whom will you share this story, when, and how?

Ask God to direct each of you to a person who he wants you to share the passage with. This can be a friend, neighbor, relative, or some person you see during the week. Naming a person and having a simple plan of when, where, how, and a few follow-up questions will make doing it easier. The first few times the family can discuss ideas of how to do this. Talk about what each person learns and give each other suggestions that will help next week. Within a few weeks these reports will become some of the most exciting parts of your time together.

- Do you know anyone who needs help? What can our family do to help them?

The last part is identifying people you can help. There are always many needs in your community. Having your family involved in helping others will add a new dimension to your family's life together. Jesus said whatever you do for the least of these, you do for him. (Matthew 25:45) Also, people are more open to hearing what you say, when they have experienced you helping them. The family projects can be short term, span several weeks, or meet some long-term need in your community.

End your time together by praying for personal needs. Then pray for each of the people that you will be sharing the passage with, and for the people that you will be helping.

LAST QUESTION — Do we need to adjust when or how we do the next study?

This last question does not have to be asked every week. It is here to make sure that your family adjusts the discovery-study time to its changing schedules with school, vacation, and holidays.

The Two Great Commandments: One of the important goals of parents is to train their children *in* the way that they should go. Jesus pointed out two Great Commandments that are the basis of all of God's requirements. The Discovery-Process introduces your children to a practical way of learning to love the Lord God with all their mind, heart, soul, and strength. Sharing the passage each week with someone who will be encouraged by hearing it, and by helping others who have needs, immerses your family in the second, "love your neighbor as yourself."

Jesus said, "If you love me you will keep my commandments" and "If you keep my commandments, you will abide in my love" (John 14:15 and 15:10). There is a growing depth of love that develops between Jesus and each of your children as they learn to obey what the Holy Spirit teaches them.

There is a **Final Commandment** which Jesus gave us, often called the Great Commission (Matthew 28:16-20). As you share these passages and what you have learned with other people, you will find some who would like to know more. As you introduce them to the same process, you will be making other disciples, which is what Jesus told his disciples to do to complete his final commission.

Specific Advice on handling children of different ages

- How old does a child need to be to be included in a family study?
    As a general rule, children under four do not have sufficient attention span to actively participate in a discovery study. From ages of four to eleven, children will enjoy physically participating by acting stories out or adding creative games.
- What can young children do while older ones participate?
    Let little children play with quiet games, joining in parts of the study that they enjoy. Even when playing they will pick up many of the things said.
- How old does a child need to be to facilitate a discovery study with the family?
    As with all advice about children, there is a lot of variability. Generally, eight-year-old children who have participated for a while,

will be able to facilitate. With some special coaching of a parent, those who want to facilitate can quickly learn how to do it.

- How do you fit discovery studies into your busy and changing family schedules?
  Busy and changing schedules characterize families with school age children. It is always best to fit Discovery Studies with existing family activities. Mealtimes, family game times, bedtimes, family devotion times, and afternoons following church services, can all be modified to include a Discovery Studies. Let older children have input and being flexible.

- How old should a child be before he or she helps start a new Discovery Group with their friends or another family?
  Once a child can prepare and facilitate a family study without guidance or supervision, they are able to help other groups start. This is usually in their later teens.

Chapter Six
Raising Children as Disciples of Jesus

As you start in this discipling process, it is useful to have a bigger picture of what you are trying to accomplish.

Matthew 19:14 – "But Jesus said, 'Let the little children come to me and do not hinder them, for to such belongs the kingdom of heaven.'"

How can we bring our children to Jesus today, not just teach them about Jesus? The first place to look is in the Bible. (In the following passages the italics are added for emphasis.)

> And Peter said to them, "Repent and be baptized every one of you in the name of Jesus Christ for the forgiveness of your sins, and you will receive the gift of the Holy Spirit. For the promise is for you and for *your children* and for all who are far off, everyone whom the Lord our God calls to himself."
> - Acts 2:38-39

> But as for you, continue in what you have learned and have become convinced of, because you know those from whom you learned it, and how *from infancy* you have known the Holy Scriptures, which are able to make you wise for salvation through faith in Christ Jesus.
> - 2 Timothy 3:14-15 (NIV)

As we saw in Chapter Four, there are families who have been using Discovery Studies for some years. They have found that these studies connect the entire family with Jesus and the Bible in a way that allows the Holy Spirit to instruct children and parents alike.

Let us start by looking at the origins of the idea of discipleship. The first record of a teacher having disciples was about 400 B.C. among the Greeks. Socrates had many disciples; the two most famous were Plato and Xenophon. The practice of discipleship traveled throughout the Grecian world. However, it was most developed among the Jews of Israel in the First Century.

Commentators have reflected on Paul's use of the phrase "in the fullness of time" in Galatians 4:4 and Ephesians 1:10. Commonly they referred to the political environment of the first century Roman Empire. This included such things as a single multi-nation government, relatively safe land and sea transportation, a highway and navigation system, common language, and common currency. It also included the development of a system of rabbis and disciples based on the Greek model. However, in contrast to the Greeks, the rabbis had a unique focus, the memorization and training in the Torah.

According to Dr. Ed Gross, there were more than 800 rabbis who had disciples and were contemporaries of Jesus. Two of them, Gamaliel, and John the Baptist, are mentioned in the Bible. Several of these rabbis had more than 1,000 disciples.

In his book *Are You a Christian or a Disciple?* [7], Ed Gross quotes Michael Wilkins[8]:

From its very earliest use (in Greek literature), μαθητὴς "mathetes" (disciple) was not simply a learner or a pupil in an academic setting. In fact, Herodotus, in whose writings the noun occurs for the first time in ancient Greek, uses the term to indicate a person who made a significant, personal, life commitment.

Socrates speaks similarly of disciples of the Spartan culture: "All these were enthusiasts, lovers and disciples of the Spartan culture; and you can recognize that character in their wisdom by the short, memorable sayings that fell from each of them."

---

[7] Edward N. Gross, *Are You a Christian or a Disciple?* (Xulon Press, 2014), https://www.youtube.com/watch?v=tUY8JQ0WkKI

[8] Michael Wilkins, *Following the Master*, pp 74-75

Ed Gross goes on to summarize:

Discipleship in the ancient world was a common phenomenon. It primarily involved commitment of an individual to a great master or leader . . . Jesus' form of discipleship was misunderstood, even by some of his closest followers. But Jesus patiently taught his disciples what it meant for them to be his kind of disciple, his kind of follower.

So, what did it mean to be the disciple of Jesus? D. Thomas Lancaster wrote:

"In the days of the Master, the disciples of the sages had four major tasks to perform:

a. To memorize their teacher's words. *The oral transmission process was the only inter-generational communication practiced among the sages . . . .*

b. To learn their teacher's traditions and interpretations. *A disciple learned how his teacher kept the commands of God and interpreted the scriptures. Every detail about the teacher was important. To a disciple, these were like gems and pearls meant to be gathered and treasured.*

c. To imitate their teacher's actions. *A disciple's highest calling was to be a reflection of his teacher. He sought to act, to speak and to conduct himself the same way in which his master conducted himself.*

d.
To raise up disciples. *He created a new generation of students and*

transmitted to them the words, the traditions, interpretations, teachings, actions and behaviors of his master.

"Many authors, while repeating the previous four characteristics of a disciple, would add one more mark of official disciples in their relationship to their teachers. It was foundational to all the rest, but absolutely necessary to be singled out and established as its cornerstone.

e. To submit completely to the will of the teacher. *First century rabbinic expert David Bivin wrote, "A special relationship developed between rabbi and disciple in which the rabbi became like a father. In fact, he was more than a father and was to be honored above the disciple's own father.*[9]

You can watch a video of Ed Gross' presentation about this at:

https://www.youtube.com/watch?v=tUY8JQ0WkKI or

www.bit.ly/EdGrossPt2

---

[9] D. Lawrence Lancaster, *King of the Jews,* pp 52-53

Jesus Modeled Disciple-Making

As you work to help your children become disciples of Jesus, it is valuable to know what that would look like. Looking at the life of Jesus as well as his expectations for his disciples, will give you a picture of what you want to see in each of their lives.

One of the primary observations about disciple-making is that only disciples can make disciples. As we look at the following passages, we see that Jesus modeled being a disciple to his heavenly father.

Obedience

"If you keep my commandments, you will abide in my love, just as I have kept my Father's commandments and abide in his love."
— John 15:10

Share from Memory

"And the word that you hear is not mine but the Father's who sent me."

— John 14:24b

Know all the Old Testament

"And the scroll of the prophet Isaiah was given to him. He unrolled the scroll and found the place where it was written,

"The Spirit of the Lord is upon me, because he has anointed me to proclaim good news to the poor. He has sent me to proclaim liberty to the captives and recovering of sight to the blind, to set at liberty those who are oppressed, to proclaim the year of the Lord's favor."

And the eyes of all in the synagogue were fixed on him. And he began to say to them, "Today this Scripture has been fulfilled in your hearing."
— Luke 4:17-19,21

"Do not think that I have come to abolish the Law or the Prophets; I have not come to abolish them but to fulfill them."
— Matthew 5:17

Imitate and Conform

So, Jesus said to them, "Truly, truly, I say to you, the Son can do nothing of his own accord, but only what he sees the Father doing. For whatever the Father does, that the Son does likewise."
— John 5:19

Make Disciples

So, Jesus said to the Jews who had believed him, "If you abide in my word, you are truly my disciples,"
— John 8:31

"By this all people will know that you are my disciples, if you have love for one another."
— John 13:35

"By this my Father is glorified, that you bear much fruit and so prove to be my disciples."
— John 15:8

Jesus not only modeled being a disciple, he also gave specific instruction to his disciples about each of these five disciplines. They are markers as you guide your children and your family to live as his disciples.

Scriptural Examples of The Five Disciplines of Jesus' Disciples:

The five disciplines that were presented in *Are you a Christian or a Disciple,* are not found as a list in the scriptures. However, they are found individually in the commands of Jesus to his disciples. They are affirmed by the disciples themselves, in how they lived. These are the disciplines that we want to apply to our own lives.

Obey Jesus in everything.

"If you love me, you will keep (obey) my commandments."

— John 14:15

"Teaching them to [obey] all that I have commanded you." [* Edit from the Greek in context of a command.]

— Matthew 28:20a

Know from Memory Jesus' commands and teachings so they can tell others.

"Have you understood all these things?" They said to him, "Yes." And he said to them, "Therefore every scribe who has been trained for the kingdom of heaven is like a master of a house, who brings out of his treasure what is new and what is old."

— Matthew 13:51–52

Know the Old **Testament** and accept Jesus' understanding of it. (Following are two examples of this.)

"Again, you have heard that it was said to the people long ago, 'Do not break your oath, but fulfill to the Lord the vows you have made.' But I tell you, do not swear an oath at all: either by heaven, for it is God's throne;"

— Matthew 5:33-34

"You have heard that it was said, 'Love your neighbor and hate your enemy.' But I tell you, love your enemies and pray for those who persecute you, "

— Matthew 5:43-44

Conform the disciple's life to that of Jesus. Most important, take on the mission of Jesus.

"A disciple is not above his teacher, nor a servant above his master. It is enough for the disciple to be like his teacher, and the servant like his master."

— Matthew 10:24–25a

Jesus' mission to reconcile the world becomes our mission.

All this is from God, who reconciled us to himself through Christ and gave us the ministry of reconciliation:

— 2 Corinthians 5:18

Make disciples following the model of Jesus — This is Jesus' final command

"Therefore [having gone] make disciples of all nations…" [* Edit from the Greek.]

— Matthew 28:19

Jesus gave us some directions that other rabbis could not. These are important in the Discovery Disciple-Making Process.

"And behold, I am with you always, to the end of the age."

—Matthew 28:20b

For he has said, "I will never leave you nor forsake you."

— Hebrews 13:5b

"For where two or three are gathered in my name, there am I among them."
— Matthew 18:20

"But the Helper, the Holy Spirit, whom the Father will send in my name, he will teach you all things and bring to your remembrance all that I have said to you".
— John 14:26-27

"But you are not to be called rabbi, for you have one teacher, and you are all brothers. And call no man your father on earth, for you have one Father, who is in heaven. Neither be called instructors, for you have one instructor, the Christ. The greatest among you shall be your servant."
— Matthew 23:8–11

Group Exercise 2: Understanding the Disciple-Making Process

Reread the preceding five sets of passages and answer the following questions:

Who is to be our teacher (ref. Matthew 23:8-11; John 14:26-27)?

What is our role in the disciple making process (ref. Matthew 23:8-11)?

Based on these preceding passages, what practical things could you do to guide your children in these things?

- *obeying*

- *knowing and sharing Jesus' teachings from memory*

- *knowing the Old Testament and Jesus' teachings about what it says*

- *conforming to the mission of Jesus*

- *making disciples*

The entire Disciple-Making Process which we have studied, is based on this: if we gather in groups of at least two or three and obey Jesus' words in the Bible, Jesus will ask the Father to send the Holy Spirit, who will help us recall and teach us all things (John 14:26).

This process is the application of promises from the scriptures. It has been tested and found true by millions of people around the world.

This is what makes this Disciple-Making Process effective! The Holy Spirit really does show up to teach, change, and transform. Jesus is the leader, the teacher, our rabbi. Each member of the family including the parents, comes as a brother or sister to encourage everyone else in the family.

The one who facilitates the study points all the members to the scriptures, not to himself. The model is Jesus, as the Holy Spirit reveals him in the words of the Bible. The Holy Spirit will do the teaching.

The model is Jesus. The words of the Bible and Holy Spirit do the teaching.

Following are three series of passages to use with your family. To establish a foundation for your family start with the Discovering God series and then progress to the Obedience series. The Parables of Jesus are an excellent place to start with small children. They are very visual, and the actions and events of the stories are easily memorized. Also, they are easy to share with other people in almost any circumstance.

Additional lists of studies are available at https://worldmissionsevangelism.com/resources/

Chapter Seven

Applying Family Disciple Making to your Church
Guidance and Opportunities

This book is addressed to families, but it can offer significant benefits to an entire congregation.

As a church wide strategy, Family Disciple Making will be more successful with supportive and pastoral care. Implementation will be smoothest if it is encouraged and introduced through a few families who are in stable living situations. The experience gained as they begin discipling their children will encourage and support other families in the church as they start family disciple-making. Think in terms of starting small and learning, then growing from the successes.

Two of the greatest benefits to the church body will be the examples of families established in God's word and the extension of the kingdom of God beyond the physical limits of the church building. Parents, children, and adolescents who are engaged in scripture as a lifestyle act as leavening for others in the church. Their regular outreach to people in their neighborhoods, schools, and places of work will produce an increasing harvest of new followers and disciples of Jesus.

At least one church has begun Teen Discovery Outreach and Youth Discovery Outreach Ministries. Ministry. Leaders working with teenagers and children, recognized that these young people from families engaged in Family Disciple Making were reaching their peers with scripture stories and starting new Discovery Groups. They began encouraging, organizing, and assisting. This has multiplied the effectiveness of these individual outreaches.

The idea of family-based disciple-making is a different way of thinking about church. Key is having a "kingdom of God" mindset. Often this is referred to as "Go" verses "Come". Roy Moran, founding pastor of Shoal Creek Church in Suburban Kansas City, in his books the *Hybrid Church* and *Spent Matches* describes blending the traditional "come" with the kingdom "go" model of church. It can be thought of as "old wine-skins" for old wine and "new wine-skins" for new wine.

Developing families who not only know about God but are living lives centered in the scriptures and empowered by the Holy Spirit will change the dynamics and future for the church. It may also change the course of our nation and society. It is part of a vision of the Great Commission.

Appendices

Following are introductory scripture passages and supplementary reading materials about Disciple Making and Disciple Making Movements.

Discovering God Series

These passages will establish a solid experience and understanding of God's plan for the world:

God Creates — Genesis 1:1–25

God Creates Man and Woman — Genesis 2:4–24

Man and Woman Eat the Fruit — Genesis 3:1–13

God's Curses — Genesis 3:14–24

God Regrets His Creation — Genesis 6:5–8

God Prepares Noah — Genesis 6:9–22

God Saves Noah and His Family - Genesis 7:1- 24

God Reestablished life on the Earth Genesis 8:1-19

God's Covenant with Noah — Genesis 8:20–9:17

God's Covenant with Abram — Genesis 12:1–8, 15:1–6, 17:1–7

Abraham Gives His Son as an Offering — Genesis 22:1–19

God Spares His People — Exodus 12:1–28

The Commands of God — Exodus 20:1–21

The Sin Offering — Leviticus 4:1–35

God's Righteous Servant — Isaiah 52:13-53:12

Jesus is Born — Luke 1:26–38, 2:1–20

Jesus is Baptized — Matthew 3; John 1:29–34

Jesus is Tested — Matthew 4:1–11

Jesus and the Religious Leader — John 3:1–21 (Numbers 21:4-9)

Jesus and the Samaritan Woman — John 4:1–26, 39–42

Jesus and the Paralyzed Man — Luke 5:17–26

Jesus Calms the Storm — Mark 4:35–41

Jesus and the Man with Evil Spirits — Mark 5:1–20

Jesus Raises a Man from the Dead — John 11:1–44

Jesus Talks about His Betrayal and the Covenant — Matthew 26:17–30

Jesus is Betrayed and Faces Trial — John 18:1–19:16

Jesus is Crucified — Luke 23:32–56

Jesus is Resurrected — Luke 24:1–35

Jesus Appears to the Disciples and Ascends to Heaven — Luke 24:36–53

Enter the Kingdom of God — Acts 2:25–41

Saved by Grace through faith — Ephesians 2:1-10

Appendices

Discovering Obedience Series

These passages will prepare your family to confront many of the common issues of life.

Matt 4:1–11 Facing temptations

Lk 5:1–11, Matt 4:18–22, Mk 1:16–2 Immediate obedience

John 1:35–51 Introduction obedience

Matt 10:16–23 Relating to unbelievers

John 15:18–25 Persecution is normal

Matt 10:23–31, Mk 13:9–13 Don't fear persecution

Matt 10:18–22, Mk 13:11–13 God's provision in persecution

Matt 5:10–12 Rejoicing in persecution

Matt 5:13–16 The life that make a difference

Matt 5:17–23 Reconciling relationship

Matt 7:17–23 Nature of sin

Matt 19:1–6 Marriage for life

Matt 5:33–37 Keeping our word

Matt 5:38–42 Revenge

Matt 5:43–48; Luke 6:27–36 Loving our enemies

Matt 7:12 Relating to others

Luke 6:27:38; Matt 5:38–42 Giving to others

Matt 6:1–4, Lk 12:33–34 Do good to please God

Matt 6:5–8 Praying with sincerity

Matt 6:5–13, Luke 11:1–4 God as Father, provider and protector; surrender, worship and forgiveness

Matt 18:21–22 Forgive always

Parables of Jesus Series

The parables of Jesus are easy to learn especially for children, although you may need to use simpler vocabulary. They can be shared in almost any conversation and quickly lead to spiritual conversations.

Matthew 13:1-9 [*The Four Soils*] (Also Luke 8:8-15, Mark 4:1-20)

Matthew 13:10-17 [*The Purpose of Parables*]

Matthew 13:18-23 [*The Four Soils Explained*]

Matthew 13:24-30 [*The Weeds*]

Matthew 13:31-33 [*The Mustard Seed and the Leaven*]

Matthew 13:36-43 [*The Weeds Explained*]

Matthew 13:44-46 [*Hidden Treasure and Pearl of Great Value*]

Matthew 13:47-52 [*The Net*]

Matthew 15:10-20 [*Defilement*] (Also Mark 7:14-23)

Matthew 18:10-20 [*The Lost Sheep*] (Also Luke 15:1-7)

Matthew 18:21-27 [*The Unforgiving Servant*]

Matthew 21:28-32 [*The Two Sons*]

Matthew 21:33-44 [*The Tenants*] (Also Mark 12:1-11)

Matthew 22:1-14 [*The Wedding Feast*]

Matthew 25:1-13 [*The Ten Virgins*]

Matthew 25:14-30 [*The Talents*]

Mark 3:22-27 [*How can Satan cast out Satan?*]

Mark 4:26-29 [*The Seed Growing*]

Mark 4:30-32 [*The Mustard Seed*]

Luke 5:33-39 [*The Fasting and patching an old garment*]

Luke 6:39-42 [*The blind man and the speck and log*]

Luke 6:43-45 [*The fruit on the tree*]

Luke 10:25-36 [*The Good Samaritan*]

Luke 12:13-21 [*The Rich Fool*]

Luke 12:35-48 [*Men waiting for their master*]

Luke 13:6-9 [*The Barren Fig Tree*]

Luke 14:7-11 [*The Wedding Feast*]

Luke 14:12-14 [*The Great Banquet*]

Luke 15:8-10 [*The Lost Coin*] "

Luke 15:11-32 [*The Prodigal Son*]

Luke 16:1-13 [*The Dishonest Manager*]

Luke 16:19-30 [*The Rich man and Lazarus*]

Luke 18:1-8 [*The Persistent Widow*]

Luke 18:9-14 [*The Pharisee and the Tax Collector*]

Luke 19:11-27 [*The Ten Minas*]

Luke 20:9-18 [*The Wicked Tenants*]

Luke 21:29-33 [*The Fig Tree*]

Supplemental Reading:

There is a growing amount of literature addressing Disciple-Making around the world. I have found the following seven books and article to be of value. These books will help your family to think about disciple-making and how they can make a difference in the world around you.

Great Commission Disciples Making, Growing Disciples Rooted in God's Word, by James A Lilly, Xulon Publishing, ISBN 978-1-4984-6060-6. This book includes a brief overview of the history of Disciple-Making Movements around the world. It is designed to guide groups of people to discover how to fulfill the Great Commission. It is intended as a training manual for teams of people who want to be part of completing the Great Commission. One of its greatest resources is the appendices. They contain additional Discovery Studies and video resources. It is available on Amazon Books.

Are You a Christian or a Disciple? Rediscovering and Renewing New Testament Discipleship, by Edward N. Gross, Xulon Press, ISBN: 9781629523491. This book will challenge you to examine all areas of your spiritual life. It is readable by adults and older adolescents.

Miraculous Movements How Hundreds of Thousands of Muslims Are Falling in Love with Jesus, by Jerry Trousdale, Thomas Nelson Publishing, ISBN: 978-1-4185-4728-8. This book is full of amazing stories that will challenge you and your children to begin thinking about the difference that they as disciples of Jesus, can make in the world. Most chapters start with a story that you can read to children who are of school age.

The Father Glorified, True Stories of God's Power through Ordinary People, by Patrick Robertson and David Watson, with Gregory C. Benoit, is based on extended testimonies about the events in *Miraculous Movements* and disciple-making in the US. This book is full of stories that children who are older than nine years old will find enjoyable.

Contagious Disciple-Making, Leading Others on a Journey of Discovery, by the father-son team of David L. and Paul D. Watson, Thomas Nelson Publishing ISBN: 9780529112200. This is written for adults who are interested in understanding how to encourage and guide Disciple Making Movements.

Spent Matches: Igniting the Signal Fire for the Spiritually Dissatisfied, by Roy Moran, Thomas Nelson, Refraction, ISBN: 9780718030629. *Spent Matches* explores the possibility that a few paradigm-shifts within the Church might make the difference between extinction and effectiveness. It is written for adults who have a concern for their local church and would like to see disciple-making integrated into it.

From Megachurch to Multiplication, by Chris Galanos describes the journey of a megachurch pastor and staff to a focus on multiplication. It addresses demographic challenges of the Church in America and one church's attempt to meet them

Article: "A Movement of God Among the Bhojpuri of North India," David L. and Paul D. Watson (p. 697ff *Perspectives on the World Christian Movement, A reader*, 4th edition (Winter, RD and Hawthorne, SC editors). William Cary Library, ISBN 978-0-87808-390-9

This article is from the textbook used in the course, "Perspectives on the World Christian Movement." For the person who wants to understand the basics of missions, I recommend that you register and take this course.

You can find information about online and local offerings of the course at: www.perspectives.org

Made in the USA
Monee, IL
10 October 2020